Monster Trucks

Blaine Wiseman

W WEIGL PUBLISHERS INC.
"Creating Inspired Learning"
www.weigl.com

Published by Weigl Publishers Inc.
350 5th Avenue, 59th Floor
New York, NY 10118
Website: www.weigl.com

Library of Congress Cataloging-in-Publication Data

Wiseman, Blaine.
 Monster trucks : WOW big machines / Blaine Wiseman.
      p. cm.
 Includes index.
 ISBN 978-1-61690-139-4 (hardcover : alk. paper) -- ISBN 978-1-61690-140-0 (softcover : alk. paper) -- ISBN 978-1-
61690-141-7 (e-book)
 1. Trucks--Juvenile literature. I. Title.
 TL230.15.S8 2011
 796.7--dc22

                              2010013937

Printed in the United States of America in North Mankato, Minnesota
2 3 4 5 6 7 8 9 0 15 14 13 12 11

022011
WEP040211

Editor: Heather C. Hudak
Design: Terry Paulhus

All of the Internet URLs given in the book were valid at the time of publication. However, due to the dynamic nature of
the Internet, some addresses may have changed, or sites may have ceased to exist since publication. While the author
and publisher regret any inconvenience this may cause readers, no responsibility for any such changes can be accepted
by either the author or the publisher.

Every reasonable effort has been made to trace ownership and to obtain permission to reprint copyright material. The
publishers would be pleased to have any errors or omissions brought to their attention so that they may be corrected
in subsequent printings.

Weigl acknowledges Getty Images as its primary image supplier for this title.
Alamy: pages 7, 17.

CONTENTS

What are Monster Trucks?

Have you ever been to a special event where trucks with huge wheels drive over cars or climb tall piles of dirt? This may have been a monster truck show. Monster trucks are big machines that use huge wheels and powerful engines to drive over **obstacles**.

Monster Jam is a well-known monster truck show. More than three million people attend Monster Jam shows each year.

Mean Machines

How do people build monster trucks? Monster trucks start out as normal pickup trucks. Special parts are added to make these trucks bigger and more powerful.

Bigfoot 5 is the biggest monster truck in the world. It stands almost as tall as a giraffe, at 15 feet, 6 inches (4.7 meters) tall, and it weighs as much as two elephants, at 28,000 pounds (12,700 kilograms). It was built around a 1996 Ford pickup that weighed 6,250 pounds (2,835 kg).

High Flyers

Did you know that special trucks can drive off ramps and fly into the air? Monster trucks are known for jumping over other vehicles. At shows, cars are lined up in a row or stacked on top of each other. Monster trucks jump through the air and crash down on top of the cars. Fireworks often explode around the trucks as they perform stunts.

The longest jump by a monster truck was made by Bigfoot 14. The truck jumped 202 feet (62 m) over a jumbo jet.

Big Wheels

How big are monster truck wheels? The wheels on a monster truck are taller than the height of the average woman and almost as wide as a small car. The wheels on most pickup trucks are smaller than the ring on a basketball hoop.

Monster trucks use farm truck wheels. These wheels weigh about 1,000 pounds (454 kg) each. This is too heavy for a monster truck, so the wheels are shaved and cut to make them lighter. It takes about 50 hours to do this.

Smash It Up

What type of cars do monster trucks crush? Monster trucks crush old cars that come from junkyards. After the cars have been crushed, smashed, burned, and blown up, they are returned to the junkyard.

Semi-trucks, ambulances, school buses, or even airplanes are used as obstacles at some monster truck shows. These vehicles are crushed at the end of the show for a grand finish.

The Race Is On

Did you know that monster trucks can be raced at special events? Many monster truck shows feature races. Two trucks speed through a course of jumps, turns, and cars. The trucks often roll over and spin around.

The fastest monster truck in the world is War Wizard. In 2005, this truck raced at more than 84 miles (135 kilometers) per hour.

Big Engines

Where do monster trucks get their power? They use normal engines that have special features. Mechanics rebuild the engine using **custom** parts. Each new part that is added helps the truck become more powerful.

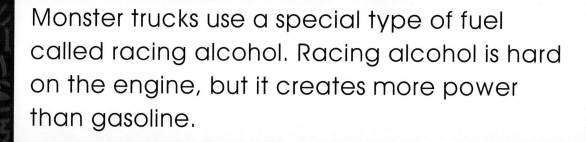

Monster trucks use a special type of fuel called racing alcohol. Racing alcohol is hard on the engine, but it creates more power than gasoline.

Truck Driver

Why do people build monster trucks? Monster truck drivers compete to build the biggest, fastest machines. They enjoy showing off the truck's strength and speed. The best monster trucks tour the world.

Sometimes, truck drivers build a new version of their truck. They improve the truck's power and size. A number is added to the truck's name to show how many times it has been rebuilt.

Monster Truck Safety

Is driving a monster truck safe? Drivers can become hurt doing the stunts and jumps they perform at shows. They wear special safety **harnesses** when they are driving.

Monster trucks have a safety device to help keep the driver and crowd safe. A computer inside the truck can sense if the driver loses control. The device then shuts off the truck's engine.

Make Your Own Monster Truck

colored pencils
or crayons

Paper

Monster Spike

1. What do you want your monster truck to look like? Look at the pictures in this book and online to help you decide.

2. Use the colored pencils or crayons to draw the truck's design.

3. Give your truck a special name. Grave Digger or Jurassic Attack are examples of monster truck names.

4. Share your big machine with your classmates, friends, or family. Tell them what makes your monster truck powerful.

Find Out More

To learn more about monster trucks, visit these websites.

KOL
http://kids.aol.com/KOL/2/Sports/PhotoGallery/monster-jam-monster-truck-pictures

Bigfoot
www.bigfoot4x4.com

Monster Jam Kid Zone
www.monsterjam.com/KidsZone

Glossary

custom: made special for a certain purpose

harnesses: safety straps that keep a driver in the seat

obstacles: objects that stand in the way or slow down movement

Index